For Bruce

Also by Doris Fiszer

Locked In Different Alphabets, Silver Bow Publishing, 2020
Sasanka (Wild Flower), Bywords Publications, 2018
The Binders, Tree Press, The Tree Reading Series, 2016

If I Were A River

by
Doris Fiszer

720 Sixth Street, Unit #5
New Westminster, BC
V3L 3C5
CANADA

Title: If I Were A River
Author: Doris Fiszer
Publisher: Silver Bow Publishing
Cover Art: "A River Runs Through It" painting by Candice James
Layout/Design: Candice James
Editing: Candice James

All rights reserved including the right to reproduce or translate this book or any portions thereof, in any form without the permission of the publisher. Except for the use of short passages for review purposes, no part of this book may be reproduced, in part or in whole, or transmitted in any form or by any means, either by means electronically or mechanically, including photocopying, recording, or any information or storage retrieval system without prior permission in writing from the publisher or a licence from the Canadian Copyright Collective Agency (Access Copyright).

www.silverbowpublishing.com
info@silverbowpublishing.com
ISBN: 978-1-77403-273-2 paperback
ISBN: 978-1-77403-274-9 e-book
© Silver Bow Publishing 2023

Library and Archives Canada Cataloguing in Publication

Title: If I were a river / by Doris Fiszer.
Names: Fiszer, Doris, 1953- author.
Description: Poems.
Identifiers: Canadiana (print) 20230522157 | Canadiana (ebook) 20230522165 | ISBN 9781774032732
   (softcover) | ISBN 9781774032749 (Kindle)
Classification: LCC PS8611.I8275 I4 2023 | DDC C811/.6—dc23

Testimonials

The poignant poems in "*If I Were A River*" by Doris Fiszer are set inside the COVID-19 pandemic. The poet navigates anticipatory grief while trying to reconcile the present with the dream logic family who haunt the nights. Amid fear and despair come touchstones: the soothing scent of lavender which intertwines with songbirds and pops of flowers. These offer solace in uncertainty, grounding and reminding us to cherish the now. The heartfelt reflection on a life's ledger insists that whatever happens, the best position is to "respond with love".

~ **Pearl Pirie,** author of *'footlights'*.

As I picked up Doris Fiszer's manuscript for *'If I Were A River'* and still then unsure of what to expect, I was immediately mesmerized by it. Its first few lines of her first poem "Origins": "I pocketed starlight before I was born / roamed the cosmos, explored the surface / of the moon, planned my beginning. // I knew by watching". And, then and there, I was hooked. That feeling never left me. I was very much taken with her use of imagery and language throughout, as in "Who Would Steal an Egg?": "hold it tenderly like a beating heart / roll it around in your palms — a cool moon // warms to the curve of your hands". This is a collection of poems centered around living and dying, family, those things we can leave behind and those we can't. It is sometimes heartbreakingly joyous. But it is, indeed, always that – joyous. It might for anyone be one of those collections of poetry you pick up and just can't put down until you've finished it. That indeed was the case for me.

~ **Bruce Kauffman,** author of *'still arriving'*.

A dreamy complement to Fiszer's debut *Locked in Different Alphabets*, *If I Were A River* embarks on a new journey of multidimensional travels through time, memory and lineage. With impact, heartache and hope, the poet offers her gift of presence in tangible mysticism as her verse unearths layers of meaning. In rhythmic glimpses through poems like "My Departed and I Travel to Bustling Cities", Fiszer captures moments with relatives in imagery that transcends worlds, interacting with them not just as phantoms, but as dimensions of herself. In this deeply attuned state, the narrator tends to their wounds, gently reassuring their voices still protectively within. Time has its own rules through the collection as it "sleeps curled up inside a tall pendulum clock/ a clock my father has stopped/ trying to repair", while intuition is the heart of the narrative. "Pay attention to your dream, Mother says". Fiszer's vision calls us to pay attention not only to our dreams, but to all the threads of connection coursing through us – to shape intergenerational experience into healed and healthy humanity through all the ordinary parts of life – soup, books, trips, children playing six feet apart during Covid – to be with what is, as gently as possible. "Now is the time for kindness / when summer is bursting — / still bursting with promise", she advises and leaves us with the wisdom of "Unfinished Landscape" to "Go straight to the purest greens", a theme she bestows to all the voices carried through her time.

~ **Cynthia Sharp,** author of *'Ordinary Light'*

Contents

Origins / 9
Isn't Hatred the Most Devastating of Earth's Upheavals? / 10
Tremors / 11
Learning to Swim / 13
Italy, 1969 / 14
Babcia (Grandmother) / 15
Visitation / 16
Babcia's Essence / 17
Visitation / 18
If You Pray / 19
Chiaroscuro / 20
Foreknowing / 21
What Does It Mean to Lose Your Mother? / 22
not wanting to wake / 23
My Departed and I Travel to Bustling Cities / 24
Waiting ... / 25
empty cup / 26
When sorrow enters your life / 27
My Night / 28
I Write Postcards to My Beloved from the Night / 29
If I were a river / 31
George and I / 32
Dream House / 33
a screen door ajar / 35
Visitation / 36
Learning to Forgive / 37
Mourning Cloak Butterfly / 38
I've Lost My Fear of Death / 39
Who Would Steal an Egg? / 40
Dream House (1995) / 41
father daughter / 42
In Lockdown the Street is Like a Glass Bowl / 43
I Follow Carolyn's Comings and Goings / 45
Grade 1V Glioblastoma: Elegy for Judy / 46
I Dream Mickey Speaks to the World
              during the Pandemic / 48
My Husband's Sixteen Days in St. Clare's Mercy Hospital,
       St. John's, Newfoundland 2022 / 49

When you were in hospital / 58
After My Husband's Lengthy Illness / 59
What Will Happen to the Music? / 60
Birthday Party / 61
all summer / 62
I linger in the doorway / 63
Unravelling / 64
Wind-blown / 65
Night Train / 66
Seeing is a Gift Not Meant to Bewitch / 67
After the Drought / 68
Black-capped Chickadee / 69
Regeneration / 70
What Became? / 71
goldfinches / 72
Solstice / 73
In the Garden without an Umbrella / 74
Unfinished Landscape / 75

Acknowledgments / 77

Origins

I pocketed starlight before I was born,
roamed the cosmos, explored the surface
of the moon, planned my beginning.

I knew by watching:
the man hovers over the woman,
his talk a warm buzz of love.

The woman arranges his favourite cookies
on a plate, stirs honey into his tea.
They hold hands walking.

I was not yet born but knew,
in this coming life,
I'd shoulder their sufferings.

Do we choose the ones who birth us?

The light I collected shone through them.
I sprinkled moon dust on their bed, my story
as worthy as any other.

Who knows how we arrive, if we carry
fragments of other lives from the blackness
like tiny scars of memory.

Isn't Hatred the Most Devastating of Earth's Upheavals?

My parents' war imprinted
in my genes —
           a shattered plate,
           a thunderclap,
           a stranger's knock.
Their childhoods weighty with the stench of sorrow.

Don't all mothers birth with courage
and silent prayers of hope,
with tender hands warm newborns' feet,
bathe infants in the same river
under the same sky?

The opposite of war —
stripping off the shutters that blind us.

And the fragrance of the garden
in early summer
before the fighting begins,
before the bricks start falling.

Tremors

1

My father's voice rumbles, a repertoire
of *Reader's Digest* jokes fills gaps
in conversations, anecdotes slide
off his tongue.

His large hands open the fridge
before and after every meal —
a biting hunger from war days.

Our arguments boil over into
the living room, his heated silences
stifle my breath until I say, *sorry*.
To restore peace, my mother says.

I navigate my father's wheel chair
through the nursing home garden,
grasp his hand to steady the tremors.

I remove the gold cross and chain
around his neck, touch his cool cheek,
my hands tremble.

2

My father dressed in suit and tie,
brown tweed cap, is running, running,
leather briefcase under his arm.
He barely glances my way.
I chase after him.

Where are you going?

I'm working, he says.

*Why do you need to work
you're dead?*

My mother stands on the front porch,
doesn't wave good-bye.

Learning to Swim

Stand tall in the water
like a warrior.
Pretend you don't hear your mother
shouting on shore or see her flailing arms.

Forget your mother's fear
of drowning,
her limp body pulled from the lake
by a man on the beach.

Start walking
until water encircles
your chin.
Keep your head above water.

Let the lake swallow
your fears —
shadows that lurk under your bed.
Let the lake take you into its depths.

Look across the water
at your father
whose body ripples
the surface like an otter's.

Suck in big puffs of air.
Kick your legs.
Paddle your arms up and down
like Zorro, your cocker spaniel.

Say sorry to your mother
again and again.
Drink in your father's approval.
You can swim.

Italy, 1969

The bus tour is a special gift from my grandmother, my Babcia. I'm sixteen. When we disembark on the crowded street in Naples, a muscular young man with wavy, chestnut hair plants himself in front of me, won't let me pass, makes lewd smacking sounds. Babcia squeezes between us. *Keep your eyes down*. Back on board, after a short stop for photos of the Amalfi Coast, he waves to me from the street. I hide burning cheeks under a wide-brimmed hat.

a red Fiat
following our bus
too closely

Babcia (Grandmother)

Nightly rituals in our shared bedroom —
you kneel in front of the bed,
pray the rosary.

You ask if I'm asleep,
don't wait for a response.

Nightly deluge of advice —
stand this way to look slimmer,
don't slump,
let your future husband think he's always right.

You retell the prank you played —
how you hid your fiancé's fedora
every time he'd visit,
your gush of girlish giggles
(the only man you'd dated,
a grandfather I wish I'd met).

You dole out your sufferings in faltering whispers —
    both parents dead from Spanish flu,
    home demolished in The Warsaw Uprising,
    husband's body in the scorched rubble,
    my mother's near death after the war.

Weighted silence when I probe further.

*

I'm dying, aren't I? you asked me.
No one here tells me anything.

You didn't bother the nurses
when in hospital.
Walked yourself to the bathroom
the day you died.

Visitation

The sky flashes —
my Babcia's face.
She offers me
her black-beaded rosary.

Don't forget to pray.

We feast on ginger ale,
freshly baked apple strudel,
all the sweetness
she denied herself
in life.

Babcia's Essence

Babcia's only indulgence —
Chanel #5

infused our phone, cutting knife,
slices of rye bread, door handles.

Ask her to stop using so much,
my father told my mother,

his short-tempered sneezes
puncturing the silence
between Babcia and him.

Visitation

Babcia takes my arm,
guides me
through a web
of corridors.

*I'll show you how
to control your father,*
she says
outside my father's
nursing-home room.

*You and he
didn't speak!* I say.

Her scent hovers
in the empty hallway.

If You Pray

Praise the darkness. Without darkness
there is no dawn.
Even the evil that lurks
in this world had a beginning.

If your prayers are answered
be grateful. Keep praying if they
go unanswered; some problems
are too large for our brief life.

When you pray, sit under an expansive tree
beside a river. Let each prayer ripple
the surface of the water like a skipping stone.
Let the earth's pulse quiet your heart.

Chiaroscuro

Rain —
collected in pots outside our small cottage,
carried in to wash my hair.
My mother's fingers lathering
shampoo and cool water,
rinsing, rinsing.
Rain
light on my head,
a cloud.

Winter walk —
fox-fur hat pulled over my ears.
Father pats my arm,
asks if I'm cold.
His breath, a white vapour,
vapour.

Babcia's rare smile —
she offers the pouch of lavender flowers
she carries in her pocket,
places it in my palm,
closes my hand around it.

Put it under your pillow when you can't sleep,
breath-less.

Foreknowing

Purple blisters erupt on my left arm.
Something's not right,

I say to my husband.
Something's wrong with my mother.

He studies the road like a tarot spread,
inches us through winter's landscape.

Trees wave their skeletons
in the blustery wind.

Faster, I say,
drive faster.

What Does It Mean to Lose Your Mother?

A sudden wind
scattered
her rose petals.

My heart twisted
into a fist —
years of blistering Julys.

Throat closed,
eyes scratched by dust,
unrelieved by tears.

Summer after summer
the clematis
withering in our garden.

*

My mother appears to me
as I twirl in my wedding dress
and white runners.

Her laughter —
candlelight
in the darkness.

She tells me to ignore
my father's words,
the biggest mistake of your life.

A week before we marry,
the clematis — a plethora of purple,
a murmur of her in the air.

not wanting to wake
      I linger
over tea with my mother

My Departed and I Travel to Bustling Cities

Father wears a backpack
bulging with Seth Thomas clocks.
Mother in fox fur wrap, ostrich feathered hat.
Babcia dances a polka in a crowded outdoor cafe.
George drives by in a red rescue firetruck.

Father tinkers with his antique clocks
in the Copernicus Hotel's foyer.
Hand me that sprocket over there.
As if I have nothing else to do.

He and I stop for lunch at the Polska Deli.
I'll pay, we say at the same time
holding up identical canvas money bags
inscribed with dollar signs.

The deli meat counter transforms into —
a revolving display of amber necklaces.
Choose one.
My father's unexpected gift to me.

George drives by in the red rescue firetruck.
Babcia dances a polka in the outdoor cafe.

Mother calls out my name
in a voice I can still hear.

Waiting ...

Lit cigarette in one hand,
red clutch purse in the other,
my mother is waiting at the bus stop
at the corner of Montgomery and Sherbrooke;
an Air Canada suitcase on the pavement.

                    Wait, I say. I need to pack.
Her voice directs, *don't forget the crystal vase;*
the one that held your first red rose bouquet
and the lint brush.
                      I cannot find my suitcase.
I throw my jeans, three summer dresses,
roller skates, a frying pan, a purple-striped hoodie
into a green garbage bag.
                      I cannot find my shoes.
I race around the apartment past crumpled sheets,
past my younger self sitting on the sofa
reading Cosmopolitan.
Uncooked porridge stares at me
with two raisin eyes in the kitchen.

                    Wait. I'm not ready,
I cry down to my mother
through the open kitchen window —
but she has vanished.
A chihuahua, tied to the cement post
is waiting ...
waiting for someone.

The scent of fresh lavender and laundry soap,
an element burns hot on the stove,
porridge cooking, its two raisin eyes
bubbles of heat.

empty cup
filled with her
conversation

When sorrow enters your life

bear the first blows
like a boxer

but allow the tears to flow.

Rest in
the lull before each round.

Shoulder grief and suffer pain,
the sparring bouts of life

but still respond with love.

My Night

is a gate I open
without dreaming.

A feral smell clings
to this sphere.

I move like a cat
charcoal prints etched behind.

I cannot hide here;
the wild releases animal cries.

No borders to arrest
the chaos of pain

I meet the dead,
arms press against me.

Our conversations
as commonplace as rain.

I Write Postcards to My Beloved from the Night
-after Margaret Atwood

1

Mother and I meander on a green
so velvety it caresses our feet
like a pair of satin slippers.

Here everything is always green, my mother
tells me, *unlike the green on earth that carries
the seeds of sorrow.*

We tour the hallway of knowledge,
shelf after shelf
laden with weighty tomes, so much to learn.
    I wish you were here to see it.

We rest in her garden overlooking
a field of swaying lilac trees,
    *You wouldn't believe
    all the brightly-feathered beauties!*

The picture of the sky, a poor depiction
of the sapphire and magenta vapours
drifting in this dream world.

The ocean, too, a washed-out facsimile.
Here the ocean breathes out waves of love.
    Thinking of you.

2

My brother is pouring a wine-coloured liquid —
"a spiritual liqueur", George explains.
    I've never tasted anything so delicious.

Mother and I — in a heart-to-heart.
Babcia places a vase of crimson peonies

on the dining room table,
already set for a family feast
in my honour.
    Though no one here needs food or drink.

Our favourite dishes —
pierogi, borscht, potato pancakes appear;
thanks before and after each platter.

Time sleeps curled up inside a tall pendulum clock,
a clock my father has stopped
trying to repair.

From here I can still see you bent over
the same book you were studying before I left.
    Miss you.

If I were a river

I'd flow between this world
              and a parallel universe
where my departed dwell.

I'd be greeted by you,
              my loved ones,
splash on shore,
              rest under another sun.

I'd restore your baritone, Father.
              Return with your sky painting, Mother.

The tinkle of voices.

Fragments of their colour-sounds
              float on my waters.

George and I

Mid-conversation, George pedals away
on a unicycle, leaves his phone
on the picnic table.

We sit around a raging bonfire,
he stacks log after log on its flames.

We sip sangria, smoke a joint
as if he were still alive.

I dial his number—
always the same busy signal.

Dream House

I don't want to live in this house —
trip on its twisted stairs, sit in the yard
littered with paint cans and empty tuna tins.

I don't want to fix the old oil furnace
that groans, sputters and stops
on the bitterest winter nights

or walk its sticky parquet floor,
or sit at my old teak desk
with the permanent blue ink stain

from my first fountain pen —
the dark sin I concealed with a blotter
from my father.

I don't want to live here
and rely on the iron with the burnt-out plug,
look out the fractured window pane

or stand under the leaking bedroom ceiling
with cupped hands
trying to catch the trickling water

or see my dead father drift in
wearing a navy suit,
I'll take care of this for you,

and yet I am here again
under the leaking ceiling,
my cupped hands, a fractured porcelain bowl,

trying to catch the trickling water
as it spatters on the floor in a brown puddle,
inhaling the same stale air.

Wandering through the dimly lit hallway
looking for the front door I never find,
I wrench my ankle on the staircase.

I fling a kitchen chair at the wall.
I don't care
if the house is watching.

Fix the furnace! Fix the leaking ceiling!
I don't care
if the house is listening.

a screen door ajar
my departed
visit in dreams

Visitation

A landscape painting
falls
off the wall,
when I bend
to retrieve it
I am strolling
down Fifth Avenue
pushing a baby carriage
every time I try
to raise the blanket
obscuring
the newborn's face
my father takes my arm,
make sure you have enough money
to pay the mortgage.

My mother hands me
a gold bracelet,
the one she lost
in Florida,
carefully wrapped
in paper towels;
a shadowy form sweeps
the floor.
I try on new clothes;
she offers
to keep my bell-bottoms,
red pleated skirt
for me.
I tell her no,
then I'll go back to making dust.

Learning to Forgive

before you speak, let your grievances lie
like cool stones in your palm

let your father exhaust deep-rooted hurts —
stubborn burrs that cling to his skin

expand your heart
let it become immense as a river

don't get tangled in a blaming web,
listen

put your ear to his mouth —
his laboured whispers

watch the clouds disperse

Mourning Cloak Butterfly

after morning rain
teardrops on my parents' grave

a yellow-rimmed flutter
on my skin
another sign from my mother

I've Lost My Fear of Death

...of all mindfulness meditations,
that on death is supreme.
    --the Buddha

I glide into dream like a bird, dreams
where my departed and I converse
without words. Boundaries blur
between earth and sky.

Here no sorrow-laden winds
or rooms thickened with cloud.

Their faces never change.
Their bodies shimmer with colour
      in a realm
         beyond the mourners,
         beyond the graves.
Is immortality etched
into every leaf?

A maple seed sails the airstream,
pollinating butterflies and bees
grace our gardens.

In death do our thoughts dissolve
like honey in hot tea,
will a kind word survive?

I've lost my fear of death
but dread the uncertainty
of its hour.

Who Would Steal an Egg?

hold it tenderly like a beating heart,
roll it around in your palms — a cool moon

warms to the curve of your hands,
its grainy shell shows its true face,

crack it open,
drop it gently into the pan,

buttery yolk, a sizzling orb,
discarded shell, shreds of prickly skin,

an egg-white mist shimmers,
gathering in soft folds,

along the road, a hungry fox,
a drifter

Dream House (1995)

Pay attention to your dream, Mother says —
    the one where I stood on the same carpeted stairs
    gazing through the window of the cathedral ceiling
    at the same flagstone patio, cedars and crabapple;
    the house that would be my own.
Put an offer on it, my father tells me
when they see it.

The night before the move
I sleep alone in my new home
on the floor under a small blanket.

Friends bring home-made soup.
Father barks at the movers —
careful with the dining room set!
(my parents' gift to me).

They assemble the children's bedframes
and mine. My father supervises.
Mother finds the kettle, offers tea.

I stand on the flagstone patio,
the stones wet with remnants of snow,
tight buds on the crabapple tree.

Judy is alone in the upstairs study
alphabetizing my encyclopedias.

I still hope to have children one day,
she says later in front of the fireplace
over a bottle of sparkling white wine.

I stand on the flagstone patio,
the stones wet with remnants of snow.

father daughter
run through sprinkler —
play puddles on the street

In Lockdown the Street is Like a Glass Bowl

1

Children wait — six feet apart
on chalk-drawn lines on the cul-de-sac.
Hopscotch. Snakes and Ladders.
Scooters. Skate boards. Tinkling bicycle bells.
The street their school yard.

Street cleaner's icy shower — washes away
their laughter.

2

Heavy rain splatters balloon bouquets—
bobbing giggling heads.
A parade of vehicles beeps horns.
HAPPY BIRTHDAY posters decorate windshields.
The neighbour across the street greets guests,
outstretched arms offer boxed cakes and gift bags.
    My wishes extended— six feet apart
under an umbrella.

3

The street, a lake after the downpour.
Bird wings splash. Dead leaves float,
paper-thin corpses. Sun breaks through cloud.
    I sunbathe in a birdcage of light
        on my front step.

4

We emerge in early evening
clanging stainless-steel spoons, handheld bells,
drums fashioned from empty coffee tins,
we inhale each other's news
like oxygen — six feet apart.

Some neighbours wave, bang pots,
call out greetings
from opened windows.

The youngest twirl and march until dusk —
sprites under street lamps.

5

Firmly taped to our mailbox —
a carefully printed note and crayon drawing
of our two homes from the two sisters in #16,

> *If you need help*
> *call us.*

6

Rose, in her kilt, parades down the street
piping *"Ode to Joy"*, *"Amazing Grace"*.
Doors fling open. Camera phones flash.
   The street, a net
that holds us, prevents us from drowning.
Applause folding into silence.

I Follow Carolyn's Comings and Goings

Her two daughters arrive in separate cars,
unload bags of provisions, casseroles and suitcases.

Self-isolating won't be a problem, Carolyn tells me
standing — six feet away on the sidewalk
in front of our semi-detached homes.

At midnight, my bedroom wall vibrates
with the hammering sounds
of tap dancing.

A jazz-tap video and photo of her transformed bedroom
appear on her Facebook page — free weights, yoga mat,
stationary bicycle, tap shoes, computer
crammed into the space.

Two vehicles park in front of her house.
I feel like Anne Frank, she yells down to her friend
through the open window.

One friend climbs a step ladder, hands
Carolyn a pulley system of knotted belts
through the opening.

The friend below places a Harvey's take-out bag
into a basket attached to a strap.
Carolyn hoists the contraption into her room.

Because I was craving a burger and fries, she posts
under the photo on Facebook, but I've caught sight
of her through the window at daybreak

pulling on her black cap, dark
sunglasses, lacing up her runners,
bolting down the street ...

Grade IV Glioblastoma: Elegy for Judy

We stop to sit on a bench in front of the river.
I button Judy's sweater, she adjusts her mask,
lifts her arms heaven-ward —

*Thank you for the ability to still walk
and still enjoy the beauty of trees.*

A silent thief has invaded her brain,
pocketed the sight of her right eye
forcing it shut like a clamshell.

Cancer treatments stretch
time — a brittle elastic.

Cards of encouragement,
a glass of bubbly on her balcony,
the scent of peonies.

Another beautiful day, she prints in her journal.

*

The robber dwells beside her brain stem,
snatches her balance,
gorges on her energy

one mouthful at a time,
growing fatter and fatter,
steals her

Montebello trip,
wedding shower,
tomorrows.

Clouds slip into her voice.
*I miss jumping into my car.
So many people taking care of me.*

One loop around the parking lot,
a rest on her walker. The skin
on her arms and legs purpled, razor-thin.

I'm

doing

all right.

*

A large lap quilt,
crafted by a friend,
warmed her feet in the hospice bed.

A photo album,
of memories, lay
on the night table.

Her name
erased
from the blackboard on the wall.

A shawl of snow covers our yard;
a wintering robin settles on a branch
in the crabapple tree.

I Dream Mickey Speaks to the World during the Pandemic

"Oh, Minnie you're all the music I'll ever need."
—Mickey Mouse

                    We need more joy —
the goodness in people's hearts sometimes hidden,
our world sombre,
a large cloud has entered our souls,
a dense fog covers everything.

                    And yet cotton candy
is still sugary on children's lips.

                    Minnie and I still stroll hand-in-hand
through Disney World and Disney Land;
memorizing the faces,
visiting the attractions again and again,
never tiring of the magic.

                    Now is the time for kindness,
when summer is bursting —
still bursting with promise.

My Husband's Sixteen Days in St. Clare's Mercy Hospital, St. John's, Newfoundland 2022

August 15. On the last day of our Newfoundland tour.

We both test positive.

A wearying taxi ride to Avalon Laboratories
to verify rapid covid tests for travel insurance.
We cannot fly back to Ottawa.

Your cheeks an unnatural red.
You cough throughout the night.
Sweat saturates your pajamas.

My night swarming with what ifs ...

August 16. Isolating at the Sheraton Hotel, 115 Cavendish Square.

You trip on the side of the bed,
push away your medications,
push away breakfast,
tell me you've already eaten.
  Where am I? you ask.
Paramedics take you to the nearest hospital.
I cannot follow.

A colourful bouquet and chocolate truffles arrive
from my family in Ottawa:
my granddaughter's purple flower drawing,
my grandson's get well note: *sorry you have covid.*

    I flap my wings, perch on the edge
    of sleep, fly over Signal Hill.
    Your hospital bedroom window open,
    I sit on the sill looking in.

August 17. Before our trip, two dreams.

> You are walking through a door,
> close it behind you.
> *Where are you going?*
> *Why can't I go with you?*
>
> I'm holding a baby.
> Its face resembles yours.
> *Who will need looking after?*

August 18. The first day I'm allowed to see you.

The month,
the day,
the time,
the place,
the sunshine,

forgotten

the minute

I step inside
your room.

Covid pneumonia and delirium, the doctor says.
Why the cane?
>Nerve damage
>*from post-shingles neuropathy,* I tell him.

You recoil from my touch
as if you'd been slapped,
as if you don't recognize me,
grimace in pain.
Your feet extend over the edge of the bed,
barely room for you to turn over.

I'm afraid to leave you.

August 19. A restless night of half-recalled dreams.

> I walk the corridors of the hotel, inhale
> the worn-out air. I open every door
> looking for the crying baby.
>
> I check our bags in at the Air Canada counter,
> place my purse on the vacant seat
> > beside me.

August 20. Nurses.

Two nurses hold you down,
another squeezes your pills
between your clenched teeth,
pushes them into your mouth.

What a workout, they say.
Perspiration splotches foreheads and arms,
flushes their faces.

Tidal waves of panic flood
my sleepless nights.
I'm terrified of drowning.

My doctor prescribes sleeping pills.

August 21. Your First Words After Six Days.

How did I get here?

I feed you Ensure (vanilla flavour),
muffin (Tim's blueberry),
toast (pb and j),
pudding(chocolate).
You sleep.

Your arm is covered in bruises
from repeatedly ripping out the IV.

You move rooms again,
the third time in six days.
(Both need painting, new dry wall
and electrical wiring).

Drilling
from next door,
the last room you occupied,
shudders you awake.

How did I get here?

I write the day, year,
the name of the hospital,
nurse on duty,
the city and province
on the white board.

How did I get here?

August 22. Detours.

Same cab driver from two days ago
drives me back from the hospital
to the hotel.
How's your husband?
Same, I say.
Don't you worry girl
he'll be fine.

Detour to the drugstore
for my sleeping pills
detour around Quidi Vidi:

A cloudless sky.
A dazzling sun.

Storm clouds teeming inside me.
No charge, he says.

August 23. Courage.

Daily phone calls, video chats, texts, emails
from my sons, stepson, friends —
their familiar voices and faces
ease worries and feelings of aloneness.

A video call from my cousin in Poland
while in hospital:
Don't worry about me, he says.
Just a strange rash and fever.
Take care of yourself, he says. *Be strong.*

Each day is another cold stone in my chest.

August 24. Breakfast.

Staff rush to deliver breakfast,
know I'm leaving early to see you in hospital.
Just the usual?
        two eggs sunny side up
        gluten-free toast
        almond butter, strawberry jam
        hot porridge, pumpkin seeds
        almond milk, mint tea, yogurt
        fresh fruit cup.

The staff member peeks in the doorway
to see if you're back.
Don't worry, luv, he'll be fine.

August 25. The weather uncharacteristically warm,
        26 degrees.

The pounds slip off me
as if I'm running a marathon.

Wrapped in layers: a woolen base,
fleece-lined hoodie, windbreaker.
I suck on cough drop after cough drop.

Fingers and toes — icy-white.
I shiver
with endless dread.

August 26. Prayers.

Walking the forty minutes to the hospital —
carrying a backpack, purse,
Tim Horton's blueberry muffin.

Name's Ernie, he says,
his LCBO bottles clink
as he wobbles towards me.
He asks my name,
where I'm going, where the park is.
He offers his bus pass, empties
his pockets inside out looking.

Do you have any spare change?
I offer three loonies and a few quarters.
I'll pray for your husband, he says
staggering towards the park.

August 27. Help.

My son and girlfriend arrive from Ottawa
for five days. They rent an Airbnb
halfway between my hotel and the hospital.
Josh visits you in hospital
the morning after they arrive.
You weep when he leaves.
He flew all the way from Ottawa.
You call him an angel.

They visit you every morning,
cook dinner for me every night.

You finish your lunch and dinner.
I'm still hungry, you say.
You make your way using your cane

from your room to the nursing station
           and back.
The nurses were surprised to see me walking,
you say, smiling.

August 28. More tests.

A nurse stops to chat while I wait for you
to have your MRI. She peers into the MRI room.
He'll be awhile. She points to the chair beside the door
the neatly folded blankets on the shelf in the hallway.
Cold in here, she says.
She opens the door to the outside,
pokes her head out, closes the door.

That's my break —
a flash of light down the corridor.

August 29. Harbourside Park, Water Street.

I sit on a bench in the park, breathe in
ocean air, exhale the suffocating
hospital smell that sticks to every pore,
feel guilty sitting here without you.

Seagulls dive for fish.
A cruise ship pulls into the harbour.
Our ten-day tour, a blur.

                I wing my way to your room,
                leave the scent of sea salt
                on your pillow case.

August 30. Celebration.

You show me how you can walk
up and down three steps.
Your physiotherapist and I applaud.
She clears you for the flight home.

August 31. Celebratory dinner.

My son and girlfriend pile my plate
with salad, steak, mashed potatoes, steamed corn.
I soak up their love.

Josh fills dollar-store containers with meals
he's prepared —
chicken, baked salmon, Habitant pea soup,
walks me back to the hotel, stacks
the fridge's shelves; they fly back
to Ottawa the next morning.

After seeing you today
I rest on the bed,
look out onto Signal Hill,
watch the fog smother the harbour.

September 1. Discharged.

While we wait for discharge papers
we play Crazy Eights,
walk up and down the hallways,
thank the staff.

At the hotel, you eat and sleep.
Our flight home confirmed,
I pack our bags,
call my stepson to pick us up at the airport.

September 2. Gifts.

I find gifts for everyone I love on Duckworth Street;
buy prepared porkchops, mashed potatoes,
pea soup at Caine's Grocery and Deli,
St. John's oldest grocery store.

You devour dinner,
are asleep by 6:00 p.m.

During the night, I dream
fog rolls in over our Ottawa street.
I forget which house is ours.

September 3. Connecting flight.

You are sick to your stomach on the plane.
The flight attendant asks me
if you'll require medical assistance
when we land.

(We only have thirty-five minutes to make
our connecting flight to Ottawa, our gate
at the opposite end of the Halifax airport).

He'll be fine, I say
> though I'm not sure if you'll be sick again,
> not sure if we'll have enough time to make
> the connecting flight.

You are wheeled to the gate
just in time for preboarding.

> I dream we are home.
> I keep checking behind me
> to see if you're there.

When you were in hospital

I sat in a room full of doctors
        dressed in starched white coats,
        lit my first cigarette
                in more than forty years,
        waited for a doctor to speak ...

I stood on a mountain wearing the linen blouse,
        the one you surprised me with,
        its yellow radiated across the lake
        glinting like midsummer sun,
        even the laces in my navy runners
        transformed into gilded strands.

I heard a melody
        notes shimmering like bird song,
        not of this world, I told you,
        how you and I danced and danced...

I tell you again
        how I looked for you on the mountain
        and in the murky swimming pool,
        crying out your name
                when I couldn't find you.

I woke reaching for your hand
        clenching only handfuls
        of darkness.

After My Husband's Lengthy Illness

I watch you digging,
your bent back shouldering
the heft of lush soil
and the slumped rose bush
that failed to flaunt her ruby reds
under the expanding canopy
of the maple's limbs and leaves.

A ball of disheveled roots and bush,
ready for resettling,
weighs on your shovel.

You rest in daylight,
set the sun-starved convalescent
in the wheelbarrow
in a gesture so tender
it trembles.

What Will Happen to the Music?

who will know
I wear wool socks to bed even in summer

who will remind me
it's time for lunch

or rest
or take my arm when I stumble

who will find me
if I wander

whisper my name in my ear
over and over

who will show me
photographs of family and friends

repeat their names
if I can't remember

or tell me
the piano that broods

in the corner is mine—
its silenced heart fills the room

will I know
it's you who sleeps beside me

Birthday Party

Maybe death is not the tragedy
we imagine, but an unsewn party dress
or black suede tuxedo jacket
that hangs in the closet, waiting ...

Each year my husband and I plan
our 100th birthday, jokesters that we are.
What we'll wear, what we'll eat,
who will need a wheelchair,
who will or will not be there.

Maybe death is an open curtain
that lets light in for those
whose bodies twist and groan
with pain or those whose minds
are prisons of fear.

Every year the guest list
dwindles. What if
I die before you, we ask.
Who will book the dance hall,
send out the invites?

Better to get our dance moves right
while we can, we say
as we hold each other tight,
as we waltz the night away.

all summer
robins' songs...
when did I notice the silence?

I linger in the doorway

of my childhood
though I've lost the key.
I linger
in all the other doorways
where I've dwelled.

The pages of the past,
crumpled on the steps,
like a rustle of autumn leaves.

My first bike,
first kiss,
wedding day,
each son's birth,
divorce,
remarriage,
loved ones' deaths,
as easy to recall as morning light
through a kitchen window.

The rest of life's grief and bliss
swirl in a gritty wind.
I'm buried in remembrances —
dreams with slanting floors,
where objects shift and vanish.

Unravelling

She remembers
the cool-blue
morning
when her
life
unraveled
like a worn-
out
sweater
she started
walking
took
what she
needed
the fibre
of her
old life
still
wears her.

Wind-blown

When he said
he loved her,
she was no longer
a shadow.

She waited for him,
a shining face
under the bridge
where the sand meets
the tall grass.

A shake of her towel,
grit razored her eyes
when he didn't come.

Her rage,
a blinding sandstorm.
Her pale extremities
hardened into pillars.

She hated herself
for loving him —
turned inside-out
with doubt
and desire.

Night Train

I sink
into the seat,
my empty home
passing
in the dark.

I close my eyes,
dive
into a deep sea,
release
the strands
that keep me
tethered
to the tattered
shoreline.

I loosen
in water's
silent music,
coast through mist
like a heron.

I follow
the tracks
of a bear
in dense forest;
flashes
of light —
maples sail by,
as if their branches
sense
the shift
to cool
a woman sweeping
her porch.

Seeing is a Gift Not Meant to Bewitch

Finding my kind,
easier than you know.
We sit on porches
and in church pews.
Forests are full
of women like us
hunting for herbs,
blending in
like a tailor's stitch.

Have I done evil?
Have I done good?
Seasons have turned
to winter.
What is real
is the cold
gripping
my wrist.

There is magic
walking in white.
A woman of my kind
has much to muse.

Which way was best?
What mode was right?
What I know
is as certain
as a whiff of smoke:
something ancient,
tormenting,
with an ominous pitch.

After the Drought

This is our earth —
parched for love
until rain streams over rocks,

pools our streets
filling the graves
of those we've lost.

We who praise the brooding clouds,
cup the first drops
splashing our thirsty gardens.

When rain continues into night
it raises us higher, returns us
to ourselves for brief moments.

We mount our thoughts
on mobiles,
hang them in the wind.

Our maps become topsails
on vessels port to port.
Festivities will prevail.

Black-capped Chickadee

Become
its sprinting
heartbeat
sing
its jaunty
song —
jazz queen
of the yard
wing your way
an acrobat —
cedar branch
to feeder
flash-splash
in the bird bath
swallow
cool rainwater
seek seed
trust
the hand that offers
watch
over offspring —
fleeting
days
like ours.

Regeneration

Inside each maple,
a record in its rings —
seasons of drought, deluge
or a forest fire scar.

Even in the driest spells
maples produce their whirlybirds.
A few emerge as seedlings,
others are eaten or decay.

Inside the body
a history in our cells —
seasons of passion and love,
disease or sorrow.

Even in the grimmest times
we give birth knowing
we carry earth's green renewal
in our human core.

What Became?

snowflake, snowflake, snowflake
no two the same

a brevity to each day
a silence before each breath

first flashes of passion
my swollen belly

I won at cards
and then I lost

I watched the maple sapling grow
robins look through the glass

ones I loved
have turned to ash

the perfect answer hangs
in the air

I wonder what became of her
we applauded each other's triumphs
saw our newborns thrive

I kept a diary then
now I wonder why

clouds with their shifting moods
still weep

goldfinches
not as yellow today
the backyard darkens

Solstice

All the singing is in my throat
as though I've swallowed a bird.
Its beating wings still fluttering in my chest.

Looking back over my shoulder
yellowed grass, the faint sun.
Ahead snow will conceal

a contemplative landscape —
the world tilts closer to the light.

In the Garden without an Umbrella

There is too much beauty in this morning —
scented with summer rain, lightweight
and idling.

Everything is as it should be —
goldfinch at feeder,
sparrow on the cedar branch,
black squirrel pecking discarded seeds.

Rain dampens my flower-print blouse,
my loosely-tied pink scarf.

The yellow iris whispers,
look at me.

Joy fills the ache of my being,
jingles in the wind.

How else did I imagine the day
would start or end?

Unfinished Landscape

Go straight to the purest greens,
ride hot summer's kiss in poppy reds,
cultivate imaginings under blush-pink days

before hues blur, blend edges
with an artist's sponge, refine
translucent blue, experiment

with the darkest darks, the shadow colours,
layer solitude with smoky gray
and midnight black, eliminate hard lines;

brace for a brittle and unresponsive
paintbrush, mounds of drifting snow
burying the grasslands.

Notes and Acknowledgements

Thank you to the editors of the following journals and publications where versions of these poems have appeared: *Feral: A Journal of Poetry and Art; Red Alder Review; Haiku Canada Review; Haiku Canada: The Trillium Haiku Group Anthology 2022-to hang my hat; Bywords.ca; The 2022 Apt613 Community Poetry Chapbook; KaDo Broadsheet 2022; Poetry Super Highway.*

"I Write Postcards to My Beloved from the Night" was inspired after reading Margaret Atwood's poem, "Postcards".

"Seeing is a Gift Not Meant to Bewitch" was initially written as a glossa prompted by Anne Sexton's poem, "Her Kind".

"When you were in hospital" was a response to Richard Siken's poem, "Scheherazade".

"My Husband's Sixteen Days in St. Clare's Mercy Hospital, St. John's, Newfoundland 2022" began as a series of hurriedly written diary entries to fill in the gaps of lost time and memory for Bruce as he recovered and as a way to manage my strong emotions when they arose. As his hospital stay lengthened, I decided to share part of our personal story in my book. Many people have been affected by the pandemic; some lost their lives; others lost loves ones. I am truly grateful Bruce recovered!

Heartfelt thanks to Candice James, publisher and editor of Silver Bow Publishing for her belief in this book. Candice's painting, "A River Runs Through It" makes a most attractive cover. Thank you!

I am grateful to Susan Gillis, poet, editor and mentor who offered insightful suggestions on all the different stages of my evolving manuscript. Her careful reading of my poems and gentle guidance brought out the best in my work.

My further gratitude to all the participants in my writing group, Ruby Tuesdays for their ongoing support, friendship and inspiration. Their constructive advice on many of these poems was invaluable in the revision process.

My thanks to Claudia Coutu Radmore who continues to encourage my writing. Her passion for haiku and other forms of Japanese poetry has stimulated my desire to write haiku. Becoming a member of KaDo Ottawa at Claudia's suggestion, has given me an opportunity to share my haiku with a small group of seasoned haiku writers and learn more about these minimalistic forms.

Love and gratitude to my family and friends for their ongoing support of my writing. As well, I will be forever grateful to my family and friends who reached out to me during our extended Newfoundland stay and after our return home. The generous acts of kindness that were bestowed upon us will always be remembered.

Thank you to my sons Joshua and Christopher who enthusiastically attend my poetry events and are delighted with my successes. They are my pride and joy. A special thank you to Joshua who flew to Newfoundland from Ottawa offering his assistance and comfort during this difficult time.

Love and gratitude to Bruce who has developed a strong appreciation for poetry, always making time to read drafts of all my poems and offer helpful suggestions. I am truly grateful for his love and his unwavering admiration of my poetry.

www.ingramcontent.com/pod-product-compliance
Lightning Source LLC
Chambersburg PA
CBHW071030080526
44587CB00015B/2559